# A MODERN FAMILY

*Keeping the Family Intact when the Marriage is Over*

To my Children and Yours

A special thanks to Scarlett Date for her
kind heart and writing genius.

# CONTENTS

# FOREWORD

I never thought I would be the type of parent who would force themselves to tolerate anything less than, to present a fake reality for anyone, including my children. Because the kids know what's going on. The same way all your friends know, when you bicker at that dinner party you regret promising to host, your kids know. Everyone has got the gist that you two are not getting along. So no, this is not a book about how to save your marriage. This is not a book on how to reignite the passion in your relationship. And this is definitely not a book about how to co-parent after a messy divorce. This is a book about how to keep your family intact when your marriage is over. That is the priority. And let's be real, faking it just doesn't work.

We have endless self-help books about how to fix our relationships. How to reignite the spark you once had. What to do when the honeymoon phase is over. Don't throw it away, make a change and stick it out. It's as though society is designed to guilt us for leaving. Divorce is more accepted than it used to be, but there's still an underlying message of, "You're selfish," for not trying harder. Especially when kids are involved. Because why would we be trying to convince ourselves to salvage something that makes us miserable? Why push through all the damage when you can find something healthier? "But what about the children?" Okay. Let's be less confrontational, let's give each other space, let's compliment each other at least once a day. Don't go to bed angry. Try to be more intimate. Let's force this stagnant, anger-filled relationship to work in the hopes that these little people who look up to us will one day be lucky enough to emulate it. We don't want to encourage them to seek something better, we want them to see what a "healthy" relationship looks like. You mustn't quit, no matter how unhappy you are. That's what they're seeing, because whether you like it or not, there's no covering the cracks. Everyone seems to forget the kids have front-row seats to this show.

It's alarming how many parents quietly resign to living in an irreparable relationship. We don't really acknowledge it as an issue. Or a mental health issue even. Is it expected, once you have a kid? A child is in the equation, so why are you any kind of priority? Your life does not stop when you have a child, nor should it. Perhaps till death do us part with the accountability of a child makes us feel forced into living it out without questioning why. The faults in an adult relationship should hold as minimal value in a child's life as possible, other than the logistics. Which is why I firmly believe in cohabiting, because the logistics stay the same, and that is all the kids should be concerned about. This personal experience and growth is what I am sharing with you in this book. On this journey, I want to equip you with the tools to stay under the same roof as your ex. Trust me, I thought it sounded crazy at first too, but it can work.

When I was finally honest with myself, I was able to verbalize the truth. My marriage was over. What's interesting were the reactions of people around me. Some of my friends with seemingly perfect relationships started telling me their truths. It seems vulnerability attracts vulnerability. A friend I'd worked with for many years, who everyone perceived as happily married, was now telling me he's miserable in his marriage. He confessed he'd wanted to and weighed out the logistics of leaving many times, but it never happened. At the beginning, he didn't leave because of the children. Then time went by and he didn't leave because it felt impossible to break up the life they had created together. Everything becomes so intertwined, cutting ties stops making sense. His lifestyle would transform into something he hadn't planned for, and for what? Now in his late 60's he is resigned to being discontent and now he really can't leave because of his wife's health issues. When did we start giving up on ourselves? Why are we okay with just being okay? Why are we willing to let piece's of ourselves die to facilitate the facade? We are not in the day and age of this or that. We fight for rights, for justice, we promote therapy. We promote self-care. We live to have it all. Unless you're a parent?

When I decided it was time to leave my husband, I had no perfect plan or idea of how it would unfold. All I knew was I'd do anything to shield my boys from the same traumas I had experienced. The faults in my parent's relationship caused me irreparable damage and cost me silly amounts in therapy. I'd love to send an invoice, but I'm an adult, working on adulting! To this day, it breaks my heart that after all the healing, my dysfunctional childhood continues to impact my self-worth. I can intellectually justify and understand, however overriding my wiring has yet to be mastered. As it does for many.

It's been over a year since I asked for a divorce and we are still living together as a family. Cohabiting with your ex when you are no longer in love, and have years of baggage, is obviously not what you imagined on your wedding day. The relationship is over, but it doesn't mean the family has to be. It takes time to adjust, and you can create a healthy reality for your children, while saving a lot of money.

A lot of things, including our relationships, aren't within our control. That's a pretty well known aspect when navigating through life. Though in true human nature, we take comfort in things we can control. And this is what cohabitating allows you to do. Your relationship may not be where you would like it, but you can choose where your family is. You can choose to work on your relationship, as parents, and keep everyone together. Neither option A. stay unhappily married nor option B. blow up your family with a divorce, are the end goal. It is a new day and age, with more possibilities. I hope my experience and this book can help you and your family to live a satisfying life.

## Chapter 1

# MONUMENTAL MOMENT

I was in the spare room lying on the bed, lights off, curtains drawn. No music, no tv, just me reflecting in my own space. I felt a false sense of comfort because the door was locked. These little locks that I'd barely bothered with had become a luxury. They provided me with the alone time I needed from Jun's frantic energy. Each night before dinner I'd come to this room for a little reset. The kids didn't mind. By the time they were done with the school day, their extracurriculars, and homework, all they wanted was a bit of screen and play time. I could hear them making a racket and play fighting in the living room. Then without warning, their joyful noise was shattered by his booming voice.

"What is wrong with you? I've had enough of this! You need to be quiet! All of you, just be quiet!"

There was total silence in the house, and it finally hit me, I feel no love for this man. I'm done. My switch had flipped, but the reality is, it's a dial that had been winding down for years. And my dial had turned all the way off, never to be turned on again. He was miserable and there was no helping him. Since we'd had the kids, he'd become very depressed and put on sixty pounds, resulting in type 2 diabetes. I tried for years to be encouraging, whether it be a simple workout or some therapy. I tried to calmly discuss why he was so angry in the hopes of working on our communication, but no. "Let's go on a dog walk, you love the dogs," but no. He was stubborn and refused any kind of change or help. All he seemed to care about was work and making sure the boys were where they were supposed to be on time. He wasn't present, he just consumed himself with the logistics.

It was May 20. I remember this because the day before was our twelfth wedding anniversary. Unsurprisingly, he had forgotten. The day drifted by with no I love yous. With no acknowledgement. It was just another Thursday. It's so odd how something so pure, being in love, can dwindle into nothing. We were once so besotted with each other that we chose to share our lives together. It's not a light decision, picking someone for life. And to make the choice to have children with someone is literally committing to them for life.

This amount of dysfunction wasn't working for anyone. Perhaps I had been in denial because I was so against separating. My parents' divorce had absolutely destroyed me in my early teens and created all kinds of hurdles in my life. At thirteen I put on a lot of weight and liked a boy who didn't, "like me, like that".. This made me an easy target, and bullying me became a fun thing to do for both the boys and the girls. As a result, I was a very angry teenager. I didn't get the care and support I needed, and this left me with a defensive attitude. Even though I matured and learned how to handle my emotions, this was now my family's narrative of me. To this day, no matter what I do, they see me as that person. I was dead against doing the same to my kids. I also realized I didn't want to be that person. However trivial it sounds, whenever I filled out a form and had to check a box—single, married, or divorced—I always felt a sense of pride and belonging when checking the married box. I felt a sense of fulfillment when completing my kids' school forms and confirming both mom, dad, and brothers all lived together. Now I would have to tick the divorced box, and I realized, I felt ashamed. I suddenly felt like a failure. But then I wondered, who was I worried about judging me? Faceless people? My friends? My family? Mostly my family. I wanted to prove to them that I had succeeded where they had failed.

At twenty-four years old, I won a trip on the radio to America."The Hollywood Experience." I decided prior to going to Los Angeles, I would stop off in New York City. If anyone has flown from New Zealand to Los Angeles, you know that New York is not on the way. I share this as it sums up my complete lack of international travel and understanding of America at the time. I was amazed to absolutely love New

York. I was like a tiger being released from the small cage she had known as home and into the jungle. When I arrived home from the trip, I immediately applied for a green card through the annual diversity lottery. To my disbelief I won, and with $600 in my pocket, I promptly moved to New York. I know that sounds insane but it is a true story. If I had not won that trip on the radio, I don't think I would have ever come to America.

In the late '90s, homebred New Zealanders - Kiwis - were very critical of the bigger is better and consumerist culture of America. I lived in a small town that only had a few TV shows and limited news sources to base our opinions on and the internet was only just starting up. My family really didn't approve of my plans. Packing up and moving to America has done nothing but feed their narrative that I'm selfish and spoiled. What with not being home to take care of my aging parents and quality time with their grandchildren being virtual, they have even more ammunition. But I could not keep living a lie to satiate this ingrained need to prove myself. The sudden pain I felt knowing my children were experiencing fear as their father yelled at them was greater than any pain I could feel from being judged.

I realized the only thing that mattered was raising healthy and balanced boys, and this was not going in that direction. The marriage was over and I had no idea what the next step was, except to go and let Jun know.

My actions were instinctual. I immediately jumped off the bed and walked through the living room, past the boys, and straight into the kitchen. They were still in silence and looked completely deflated. I shut the door behind me and told Jun to stop being so angry toward his family. It was emotional abuse. He didn't acknowledge me. I proceeded, the words spilling out, "I am done and I want a divorce." Unsurprisingly to me, he was dismissive and stormed off into the garage. This was the moment, monumental to me, and miniscule to him.

My marriage had fallen to pieces. I had spent the last four years feeling like a single woman, minus the agony of first dates. I had the mindset of, "You've made your bed, now lie in it." I would still have sex with my husband but my heart wasn't in it. I was constantly trying to stay focused on what I had to be grateful for. This also helped me to remove myself emotionally when Jun was angry and stomping around the house, which was most of the time. The kids were scared of him and I was so lonely and despondent. We were also broke, as we had been for most of our married life. Neither of us had come into the marriage with money. And having met whilst completing our master's degrees at the University of Southern California, we had a large amount of student debt burdening us. Even though we both worked, we still lived above our means. This is easily done when living on the westside of LA, especially after having three children back-to-back.

We were finally climbing out of our financial hole when the pandemic hit, and I had to shut down my consulting business.

I specialized in workplace conflict, and well, no one was in the workplace anymore. We were now at the tail end of social distancing and virtual schooling for two years and without any real space from each other. Jun and his sister both worked out of the garage that was attached to the house. I had come to despise Jun at times. But in true honesty, I felt very little for him a lot of the time. Both of us mostly ignored each other. It seemed I had become numb to everything but the occasional bout of massive frustration. I had lost all respect and all feeling otherwise.

Due to the pandemic and social distancing, the kids had been playing a lot of baseball. We had three boys on two teams each. It was full on and we would spend days on end in the bleachers, cheering the boys on. Except Jun's idea of cheering them on was yelling unhelpful criticisms from the sidelines. It wasn't productive, and despite me repeatedly asking him to stop, he wouldn't. It started to get embarrassing, I'd cringe every time he opened his mouth and the other parents started to stare.

My parents had a really terrible divorce, like so many couples I knew and read about. I never wanted to do that to the children. Clearly, no one thinks they are going to get divorced when they get married, even though in the United States over 50 percent of marriages end this way. It seems the fairy tale and myth of living happily ever after overrides logic. Still, it happens to the best of us. However, I did factor in logic when deciding on the father of my children. Jun was so kind and he had such a gentle heart. I remember when we first started dating, I had a dog and two cats who would sleep on the bed with me. One night when Jun slept over, I overheard him politely asking my cat Harold if he could please move over. It was so sweet. It's little moments like this that mean everything. He was a keeper and I knew that if anything ever went horribly wrong, he would do right by the children. I felt he didn't have it in him to hurt them. It turns out that even though it was touch and go for a while there, during a particularly tumultuous time, he has proven me right. He is still 100 percent committed to the children and to me. Despite all his blunders, Jun's dedication to this family has been outstanding. When we stopped having sex, he remained committed to me. When I told him I wanted a divorce, he remained committed to the family. And when I moved out, he decided to come with me to live together, but separated.

Although Jun's commitment to the family has been unwavering, before the separation he was putting too much value on physically being there and not on the quality of the time spent. His parents had not been available to him as a child, physically or emotionally. They both worked six and a half days a week. Jun was brought up by his grandparents who were very old school in their values, and this resulted in him not having any emotionally available role models. So he put the most value on being physically available, no matter in what state of mind, without second guessing it.

When his behavior started to impact the children, I decided I needed to be honest about the state of our relationship. I could no longer convince myself that this was the best for our children. It wasn't. Divorce is far from ideal, but neither is having your sons learn terrible behaviors from witnessing their parents' unhealthy relationship. The boys were eight, ten, and eleven, so I decided I needed to take action now. In a few more years they would be full of hormones and less inclined to talk to me about their feelings or worries. What teenager wants to talk to their parents, let alone have a heart-to-heart? When my brother and I went through my parents' divorce, our sudden big feelings weren't within our capacity to manage, which led us to drugs and alcohol. And I really didn't want my boys pursuing unhealthy outlets because I didn't manage the situation the best I could.

If you are still questioning if there is hope to rekindle your marriage, below are some common indicators that suggest a relationship may be beyond repair:

1. Emotional Disconnect: You no longer share your feelings, dreams, or daily happenings. The emotional intimacy that once existed has dwindled or disappeared.
2. Lack of Physical Intimacy: A significant decline or absence of physical closeness, like hugging, kissing, or sexual activity. Especially if it has been ongoing and is not due to a specific circumstance.
3. Avoidance: You find reasons to spend less time together, avoid coming home, or engage in activities that keep you apart.

4. Indifference: They have begun to feel like a roommate.
5. Constant Conflict: Arguments are frequent, and resolution seems impossible. The same issues are rehashed without any constructive outcome.
6. Avoidance of Conflict: On the other end of the spectrum, a complete avoidance of conflict or an apathetic attitude toward disagreements can also be problematic.
7. Fantasizing About Life Without Your Partner
8. Breaking Trust: Infidelity, lying, or other breaches of trust can seriously damage the foundation of a marriage.
9. Lack of Respect: Consistent feelings of disrespect or being disrespected can be corrosive to a relationship.
10. Different Life Goals: Over time, if partners develop
11. vastly different visions for the future (like whether to have children, where to live, or career aspirations) and can't find a compromise, it can lead to irreparable rifts.
12. External Affirmations: If either partner is seeking validation or affection consistently from sources outside the marriage, it might indicate a lack of fulfillment within the relationship.
13. Reluctance to Seek Help: Refusing to attend couples therapy or dismissive attitudes toward getting help might suggest a lack of commitment to repairing the relationship.

14. Abuse: Any form of abuse—emotional, physical, or psychological—is a clear sign that the relationship is toxic and harmful.

I don't know about you, but when I put that list together, I felt reassured that my marriage was over. The only bullet point that didn't apply to me was having different life goals. We still had and have the common life goal of raising healthy, happy, and well adjusted boys.

Chapter 2

# EMOTIONAL STAGES

During the breakdown of a marriage, one person is typically further down the road, emotionally. More often than not it is the wife, as statistics say that 70 percent of divorces are initiated by the woman.

I didn't think it would be such a shock for Jun. I had told him once before that I was done, but I didn't truly believe it myself, so neither did he. With the false words, nothing changed. The next time I told him, I meant it and said it with conviction. This time it sank in. With this came a problem in our different stages of acceptance. I had emotionally moved on, the relationship was done, and I was aware of what was missing. Whereas Jun was in denial. There was now no crying on my end, because all my grieving had come and gone. For Jun, there was a lot of crying and he was on an emotional rollercoaster that I couldn't keep up with. I just watched with a mixture of dread and sadness, trying to protect our children from his erratic behavior.

I wanted to discover how we were going to make this work with minimal emotional damage to the children. We were in such different places emotionally, I had to be extremely patient as he processed his pain and went through his own grief. I know that while he was processing this, if I had physically left him, we would be in a completely different place now. Going through it as a family I believe showed the children that as a family we are resilient and we can all do crazy things, but we will always be loved.

In the early days, after telling Jun the marriage was over, he was so angry. It would come out in unpredictable and manic waves. Especially when he was drinking, which he was doing a lot of in the beginning. He would follow me around the house, getting in my personal space, shouting things like, "You can't leave me, I won't agree to it!" He even picked the lock to my room late one night. I was fast asleep as he used my thumbprint to unlock my phone and go through it. Pretty sure that's illegal! And on this investigation he found a text from my brother, Blair, that upset him. So he called Blair and ripped into him, lighting that bridge on fire.

This suspicious and particularly angry behavior came about because he was not on board with the idea of divorce. At first his rationale was that I couldn't leave him if he refused to leave me. After some time in this state of denial, he then decided if he couldn't be married to me, he would kill himself. He was suicidal for weeks. He kept oscillating between crying and shouting at me and self-medicating with alcohol, staying mildly buzzed for weeks. It was terrifying. I was able to convince him of a temporary compromise until he sorted himself out. He needed to get his own apartment. I thought it would be the best for all of us. He needed his own space, somewhere to retreat to when he was feeling out of control. He'd have some time off from the everyday demands of the kids, and his own space to reset it. Luckily, my friend Claire recommended a property manager who helped us find somewhere convenient for that time. It was tiny but furnished and we could rent it from month to month.

Again, Jun was not on board, but he couldn't disagree. He was an emotional wreck and his anger wasn't conducive to a healthy reaction from the boys. In moments of weakness, he would say to the kids that Mommy wanted a divorce and didn't love him anymore. These weren't healthy discussions and I resented him for it, but it's done now. It was part of his process. We don't always have the right reactions, but that's life. The kids were understandably really upset and worried about whether there was truth in Jun's words. I couldn't deny what was happening and I didn't want to give them false hope, so we had to talk it out. It seemed I was back to where I had started as a child, mediating a divorce. Being the adult in the scenario, that was okay with me. In an attempt to keep the peace, I told them that their dad just needed some space and to get a handle on his emotions. This is a more adult-type conversation than I would have cared to entertain at their ages, but it beats the alternative of them wondering and festering.

The day he moved out, it was a long goodbye. He had two plastic containers with his clothes at the door but he wouldn't leave. It was so unnecessary and painful for the boys. It made it confusing. He finally left at 11 p.m. but was back the following morning at 6 a.m. This became his pattern. He'd moved out but it felt like he hadn't. Aside from sleeping somewhere else, he was always in the house. On his part, this was a massive fail. There was no way to influence his actions, no matter how healthy my suggestions that wouldn't make the situation go nuclear. I tried to stay out of his way but this was not easy, as our house was small and he was still working from home. This was his routine until he stopped going to the apartment altogether. After only a couple of weeks, he started crashing on the couch at the end of the day, essentially moving back in.

Feeling pushed into a corner, I suggested we take turns staying at the apartment, which he didn't really go for. He tried it a handful of times but it didn't take. I kept my end of the bargain and stayed at the apartment a few nights a week, to see if that would help decompress the situation. I came up with a plan that the kids could take turns between the house and the apartment to have one-on-one time with both of us. However, I think being in this indefinite uncertainty made them crave security, and they wanted to sleep at home. I can't blame them. When you feel out of control, you hold onto anything you know.

At their insistence, they also wanted me there first thing in the morning and last thing at night. I'm assuming it was for consistency or perhaps in a bid to see their parents in one home. Whatever their reasoning, I accommodated. Now neither Jun or I were using the apartment and it became a worthless financial drain. Admitting defeat, we gave notice to the property manager and were back in the same toxic environment that I was trying to move us on from. It was so frustrating, his refusal to even try. I wanted him to take a step back from the relationship, process his therapy sessions and calm down in his own space. But his stubbornness wasn't driven by logic, but by his all-consuming rage.

After this failed attempt for some space, I resigned myself to the fact that I'd have to leave Butler Avenue and the kids would have to go back and forth between two places. I started looking for a second house but was struggling to find anything that was up to par or close to where we currently lived. I knew it would have to be comparable for the kids to feel settled. However, being in no rush for the kids to only spend half of their time with me, I wasn't going full steam ahead. I couldn't even get my head around the idea. It was early August and I realized I didn't have it in me to build my business back up. Instead, I started a senior-level role at a finance company in downtown LA and was now making a substantial and regular income. So I was going to push pause, continue to live together but separated, and start saving up. Setting my sights on moving out by the end of the year, I had a few months to build myself a little nest egg and find the best second home for the boys and me.

**Exercise**

A little confidence in yourself, and back up, goes a long way. Turning to your support network can help with this. That said, if you don't have a supportive network that makes you feel seen and connected, now is the time to start building one. I joined my local Rotary Club and found an amazing group of people who were not affiliated with any religion or politics, their only focus was on doing good in the world. This group of people was there for me when I needed support. They helped me network, I had new resources, new opportunities, and a safe place to go where I was cheered on. To me, that was invaluable.

Take a moment to think about who is in your network that brings positivity into your life and will have your back when needed. Also, think of the people who are less positive, who you may need to distance yourself from when you are feeling vulnerable. If you could do with more supportive connections, now is the time to start putting yourself out there. What you are going through is not easy, the road is going to be bumpy, and having people to back you up is a game changer.

This week, find one thing you could do that is outside your usual routine, to start strengthening or building your connections.

Some of my examples are the Rotary Club and reconnecting with friends who had drifted away due to life getting in the way. Also pre-kids, I had been quite active in a professional group for mediators. In an effort to keep these relationships, I restarted my membership and started attending some of their events. It was refreshing to see old, familiar faces. I had forgotten how much we had all done together over the years and the connections were easily reestablished.

Chapter 3

# DIVORCE AND DENIAL

Fear is a huge part of why people stick to the familiar, even when it totally sucks, what we know feels safer and we are biologically wired to seek out safety. Dysfunctional relationships seem to be winning over the unknown, because trusting the process when you have no idea how it will fall into place, is terrifying. This fear creates resentment, because you want to leave but feel like you can't. More often than not, the relationship will eventually become so toxic that you end up despising each other and the family's foundations are left in ruins. When your choices are driven by fear you will never know true freedom, because the choices you make are not coming from what you value. In this book, I want to help you find clarity on what decisions are more true to what you value, so you can make the decisions that bring you true freedom.

Before the marriage was finally over for me, I had been resigned to living in a loveless one.. I wanted my children to have an intact family, and it seemed the best means of providing this was staying together, no matter how unhappy we were. We all want to set up our children to succeed, we want them to have an ideal childhood, and we know how vital those first years are. In fact, I read a statistic that by the time a child is of age 12, we would have spent 75 percent of the time we will spend together in their lifetime. With facts like this, the possibility of me pursuing anything other than an unhappily married mother was so unfathomable. It's crazy the sacrifices you'll make for your kids. Family is everything, my kids are everything, but when things don't go accordingly, it's so easy to feel trapped and fearful.

My parents came from a generation where divorce was uncommon. Typically the mom stayed at home with the kids and the husband worked. That ol' "bring home the bacon" type of life. There was a lot of shame behind divorce and few examples of how to do it successfully. Again, resources and research were scarce. Women around us, or any of reference, lacked financial power and fell victim to societal expectations. Everyone prioritized a happy family over a happy individual. This is what threw me even more, when my parents sat my brother and me down to unload the truth of their situation. And I think because it was so taboo at that time, it was handled poorly. Which is why I feel so inclined to share my story, because with more awareness comes better decisions.

Initially, my parents tried keeping my brother and me in the family home, and they would take turns staying in the house with us (nesting). This might have worked, except my dad was now in a full-blown relationship with Betsy, the woman he cheated on Mom with. Betsy would come and hang out at the house and sometimes sleep over; this drove my mom bananas. Betsy was in her house, in her garden, and with her children. This dynamic became unbearable. After six months my parents agreed to make the financially unsound decision of selling our house in the country. They split the pie and we went from being upper-middle class to lower middle class. Dad moved to a tiny, tatty apartment with a miserable roommate, and Mom's boyfriend built her a prefabricated house on a tiny lot by the school.

Divorce is currently a multi-billion dollar industry in America. That means there is a lot of money to be made from people who are traveling this rocky road. Over one hundred million people are currently married in the United States, and approximately 50 percent of these people who are in their first marriage, will divorce. This rate only increases with the number of times a person has been married. Divorce is a massive financial and emotional cost to you and has an incalculable emotional cost on your children. Who wins? The Lawyers.

Litigation is a lose-lose situation. You will be hard-pressed to find anyone who walked away from a divorce that involved lawyers, courts, and costs, who felt like they'd won. Any financial win that drains the marital pot will pale in comparison to the trauma the family will endure in the process. Ultimately, lawyers sign an oath to rigorously advocate for their clients, and this can lead to a limited focus on all that can go wrong, all they are protecting their client from, and framing the best deal. Which is what you want in most areas of the law, but not in family law. This approach can perpetuate fear, mistrust, and miscommunication, often leading to a drawn-out process that can leave an already fragile family in pieces.

The opposite is needed during the uncoupling of two parents. Trust and communication needs to be rebuilt, and since the end result is two households, you should be saving every penny. And during this time, the priority should always be the children and their needs. That is why you're even contemplating staying in the same house. But when the legal system is left to prevail over a family, it is now up to "experts" to decide what is best for your children.This is madness, and if you believe the legal system is set up to know better than you, what is best for your child, I suggest the book, I Just Want This Done: How Smart, Successful People Get Divorced Without Losing Their Kids, Money, and Minds by Raiford Dalton Palmer. This book goes into great detail on how broken the legal system is when navigating a divorce with children.

The dissolution of the marriage is a phase in your family's lives, not an ending. So let the way you go through this phase set you both up to successfully parent your children with no additional pain, suffering, or obstacles. As tough as it is that your marriage isn't working, you get to influence how much conflict you will allow into your relationship. It's important to note that not all conflict is detrimental. Occasional disagreements, when resolved in a constructive manner, can teach children valuable life skills. This includes negotiation, empathy, and resilience. However, chronic and unresolved conflict—especially when it involves aggression, hostility, or violence—will have only negative effects. This can affect their emotional, behavioral, social, and even physical well-being. The effects can vary based on the child's age, temperament, and the nature and intensity of the conflict.

Here's a summary of the potential consequences:

Emotional and Psychological Impact:

- Anxiety and Fear: Children may constantly be on edge, fearing the next outburst.
- Depression: They may feel helpless or believe they are the cause of the conflict, leading to feelings of guilt and sadness.
- Lower Self-esteem: Prolonged conflict can make children feel they are to blame or that they are inadequate.
- Stress: Chronic stress can lead to various health problems, both mental and physical.

Behavioral Impact:

- Aggression: Children may act out and become more aggressive or hostile.
- Withdrawal: Some children retreat from family and friends, isolating themselves.
- Academic Issues: They might struggle in school due to distractions at home.
- Substance Abuse: More so in adolescence, some children turn to drugs or alcohol as a coping mechanism.

Social Impact:

- Trust Issues: Children might develop problems trusting others, impacting their ability to form healthy relationships.
- Poor Social Skills: They might struggle with conflict resolution or become more aggressive or withdrawn in social situations.
- Replicating Behavior: Children often model what they observe. If they see conflict as a standard way of interacting, they might repeat that in their own relationships.

Physical Impact:

- Sleep Issues: Anxiety and stress from parental conflict can lead to sleep disturbances, ie., bed wetting

- Health Problems: Chronic stress can contribute to health issues such as headaches, digestive problems, and weakened immune systems.
- Developmental Delays: In younger children, constant stress might lead to delays in certain milestones, growth, speech, etc.

Cognitive Impact:

- Impaired Concentration: Continuous thoughts of problems can reduce a child's ability to focus on tasks.
- Problem-solving Skills: If children are exposed to only confrontational resolutions, they might struggle to develop effective and peaceful problem-solving skills.

Long-term Impact:

- Relationship Difficulties: Adults from high-conflict homes may struggle with forming or maintaining romantic relationships.
- Mental Health Issues: The psychological effects of parental conflict can continue into adulthood, increasing the risk of mental health problems
- Parenting Challenges: When they become parents, they are likely to replicate the patterns they observed growing up, continuing the cycle of conflict.

Unsurprisingly, due to my childhood, I sought out a career in mediating divorces. I even have a masters degree in dispute resolution. I wanted to help people protect their children from the craziness of divorce. That lasted about six sessions and I was out. One couple I worked with had caused irreversible damage to their relationship from the amount of conflict caused by their divorce. It was tragic to witness. By the time they were in court-mandated mediation, they had totally lost focus of what was important. They had four-year-old twins and the father was a lawyer, and the judge had told him that he was not allowed to spend another cent on his divorce. He needed to either settle it in mediation or the judge was going to make a final ruling on it. No more delays and no more money. The divorce had reached one million dollars and the wife didn't have a job and was completely at her wit's end. I felt like yelling at them, "You have to parent these children for the rest of your lives! This is not the means to an end, you're in this forever, what are you not understanding?!" This was a big part of why I hated divorce mediation, it was too personal for me. Staying neutral? Heck no, I was so opinionated. Sometimes I had to excuse myself. How many great divorce stories have you heard? I'm sure you've heard a lot more horror stories. Because the system is designed to put money in everyone's pockets but the couple. So yeah, no one lands on divorce lightly.

As I mentioned earlier, once I was able to admit the level of dysfunction in my marriage, other people's truths started spilling out. Seemingly happy and well-functioning couples were telling me their very real and disheartening problems. Apparently, I wasn't the only one presenting a false reality. I took a slight comfort in knowing I wasn't alone in pretending, but found it troubling that this was the norm. A lot of the time it feels easier to stay than to leave. The longer a marriage drags out, the harder it becomes to cut ties. And of course, there's the overwhelming fear of dying miserable and alone. Yes, that little worry!

Here is a list highlighting the common reasons other than the children, that people stay in dysfunctional marriages, do any of these resonate with you?

1. Financial Dependence: One partner may be financially dependent on the other, lacking the necessary resources or job skills to solely support themselves. This dependence can make leaving the marriage incredibly difficult, especially if children are involved.
2. Social and Cultural Pressure: Societal norms, family expectations, and cultural pressures can strongly influence a person's decision to stay in a marriage. Even if it is unhealthy. Stigma around divorce can create an environment where leaving feels wrong.
3. Low Self-Esteem: Individuals with low self-esteem may feel undeserving of a healthy, loving relationship. They might tolerate abuse or neglect because they do not believe they are worthy of anything better.

4. Hope for Change: Many people stay in unhealthy marriages with the belief that their partner will change. This hope can be fueled by intermittent positive behaviors. A cycle of apologies or promises to improve, which may never come to fruition.
5. Religious Beliefs: Some religions strongly discourage or condemn divorce. People with strong religious beliefs may feel compelled to stay in an unhealthy marriage to adhere to their faith's teachings, fearing social ostracism or eternal consequences.
6. Fear of Retaliation: In abusive relationships, the fear of retaliation—whether physical, emotional, or financial—can be a significant complication. Abusers often use threats, social isolation, and intimidation to maintain control over their victims.
7. Lack of Awareness: Some individuals may not realize that their marriage is unhealthy, particularly if they have grown up in a similar environment, or have not been exposed to healthy relationships. They might not recognize the signs of abuse or manipulation.
8. Emotional Dependency: This occurs when one partner relies heavily on the other for emotional support, often to the detriment of their own well-being. This type of dependency can make the thought of leaving so daunting, as it would mean losing their primary source of emotional support.
9. Practical Reasons: Some people stay in unhealthy marriages for practical reasons, such as shared assets,

children, or health insurance. The logistical challenges of separating lives can seem overwhelming, especially if the marriage has lasted for several years.

10. Fear of the Unknown: Leaving a marriage, even an unhealthy one, can be terrifying due to the uncertainty that lies ahead. Fear of being alone or starting over can be paralyzing and keep individuals from taking steps toward a healthier life.

If any of these reasons apply to your situation, I recommend working closely with a therapist to decide what alternatives there are and if cohabiting is an option for you.

## Chapter 4

# CREATING YOUR IDEAL LIFE

Creating a vision for your future, even as uncertain as it may seem in your current situation, is something that carries power. Especially when you include how you want to feel and what you want to see. To (mentally?) lift yourself out of your current situation, I would like you to write down what would be your ideal living situation. Think about every aspect of this scenario. Not just how it presents, but how you feel, how your children feel, and how they are behaving. Don't let the reality of your situation limit your vision.

Here is mine:

I am healthy and happy, as are my children. We live in a spacious house in Southern California, with lots of light. I own my home and it has zero clutter. I feel calm and in harmony as I sit at my desk looking out towards the ocean.

My three children spend a lot of time together, laughing and playing games inside and outside. The boys do their homework in the front room, and because of the big table, they can spread out and work together. They are so happy and kind and still want cuddles at night. There is a big pool, where we spend a lot of family time. My boys are kind, thoughtful, and grateful for all their blessings. They thrive socially, in school, and on the sports field.

Jun and I live with our new partners, who both love the kids. We regularly have big joint family dinners at my house and his. We laugh around the dinner table all joking and smiling. The collaboration between our two homes is seamless. There is no animosity or tension, it's easy. I occasionally travel for work and when I am away, Jun happily has the kids. And vice versa. We also have a group of close friends with whom we take family trips.

Now it's your turn. Pick up a pen and take a moment to fantasize,

________________________________________

________________________________________

________________________________________

________________________________________

________________________________________

________________________________________

Now read over what you just wrote and pull out what values you identify. Then, given your current situation, rate each value out of ten.

From my example, the values that I believe my perfect life identifies are below, rated by where I was before cohabitating.

| | |
|---|---|
| Intimacy | 0/10 |
| Harmony | 2/10 |
| Communication | 1/10 |
| Joy | 1/10 |
| Fun | 2/10 |
| Kindness | 2/10 |
| Adventure | 1/10 |
| Finances | 3/10 |
| Division of labor | 3/10 |

________________________________________

________________________________________

________________________________________

________________________________________

________________________________________

________________________________________

________________________________________

________________________________________

________________________________________

This exercise is to put your situation into perspective. It's an important part of the process to know where you are in regard to what you want. This will help place your focus on the right things and reach an outcome that suits you. Obviously, you are reading this book because your marriage is struggling or already over. This would suggest that most of your current value ratings are low. Now think about what needs to change and what you can control to bring those numbers up.

For those of you with really low numbers, who are still pretending the relationship isn't over, can you ask yourself why? Is it the logistics of moving out? Is it as simple as being too comfortable? Is it because your partner has high-conflict personality and you are afraid of the destruction that will ensue once you make your move? Your reason might not just be for the kids and it is legitimate. This is why a clear distinction of what you value and want in life is important, so you can make any decision with confidence.

For those of you suffering abuse, I don't have all the right words to help you. I do know that you need to find a way to leave, and I strongly recommend seeking all the professional help you can get. An aspect of domestic violence is that your partner slowly erodes your support system. You probably feel alone, but there are people out there who can help. Perhaps start with counseling.

So let's talk about if you are paralyzed by your next move. Perhaps you can't see past option A or B? If there was an option C, separate but live together, what would have to change between you and your spouse? How would you need to alter your parenting styles in order to achieve this?

You may not have faith in the process right now because you're deep in the trenches of negativity and dysfunction, but give it time. I was there too but it can work. Have some patience and commit to the cause,—I promise it's worth it. But know, it will not happen overnight.

**Exercise**

List what needs to change and what are some actions you can take to have a healthy home life.

Here are a few of mine:

- Spend more quality time with the boys
  One on one time
  Walks
  Read together in the evenings
  Spending longer at the dinner table
- Be kinder and more patient with Jun
  Leave the room if I feel agitated
  Go to bed before I am over-tired
  Don't have a conversation in the morning before Jun has three cups of coffee
- Etc

What I need from Jun, I have no control of this but it's worth a try:

- Control his temper and stop taking his anger out on his family
  Leave the room when he is stressed and feeling angry
  Go for walks
  Don't try to communicate when he is angry
- Learn how to respectfully communicate with me
  Learn how to use the Non Violent Communication framework when he is angry
- Etc

___

___

___

___

___

___

___

___

___

___

___

## Chapter 5

# WHAT IS BEST FOR THE CHILDREN

In the midst of his sadness, Jun started having suicidal thoughts. His emotions drove him to think that living without me was worse than living for the kids. After a stressful and emotional exit one night, I was driving around looking for him. He was very drunk and had told me he was going to kill himself. It didn't feel like some call for attention, it felt like he really meant it. The evening had started with a big fight, fortunately, the kids slept through it. Then, after a lot of going back and forth, I went and sat in my room and heard him leave.

On top of the stress, I was so angry with him. Why was he prioritizing a relationship, our relationship, over our children? I wasn't, they were still my priority. Yes, this emotional transition wasn't new to me but never in any stage would I have thrown away their needs because of mine. He was reminding me of my dad and I hated it. This wasn't the man I had married. He was proving my reasoning for picking him as a father wrong. Their dad, my children's dad, was about to devastate them because he was so preoccupied with his own emotions and life. The relationship had dwindled into nothingness and because he couldn't see this, he was going to ruin our children's lives too.

A parent committing suicide creates unimaginable trauma for a child, especially young ones. And if my kids were to find out that Jun blamed me, it would be extremely detrimental to all of us. Not only would they have lost their father, they could potentially believe me to be the reason why. I knew it was something none of us would recover from. He was threatening to inflict more harm than I could ever have imagined and it was a complete annihilation of our agreement as parents. I was wild, then I started feeling scared as the terror crept in. I grabbed the keys, locked my sleeping children in the house, and jumped in my car.

I knew he was on foot and couldn't have gone far, but after an hour, I wasn't sure what to do. No one prepares for these situations, you're not taught what to do. We learn English and algebra at school, not how to chase a suicidal husband around the streets. So I called my cop friend, asking if I should call 911. He ran through the possibilities with me and mentioned the backyard. I hadn't thought of that. Why make this big spectacle, only to sit in the backyard? Apparently it's a common practice. He told me to go home and check. Much to my relief, he was asleep in the garden. I wanted to cry and shout at him, but instead, I left him to sleep outside. I was exhausted and had to get up and go to work in a few hours.

Once the only reason to stay together becomes the children, there needs to be a constant assessment of whether the situation is really what's best for the children. You and your ex modeling healthy behaviors and being emotionally and physically available to your children is what's best for them. If you are unable to maintain a healthy relationship, then the answer is no, it is not best for the children. This whole process needs to be driven by that one question, is this what is best for the children? Because the moment it isn't, something has to change.

Statistics say that 68 percent of parents who divorce with children still living at home regret parting and wish they had tried harder. Thus, continuing to live together in this way for a little longer, can be a valuable part of the process. I am not saying stay longer to see if you can fix your marriage, I am saying give yourself permission to be honest that the relationship is over and still stay, this gives you permission to be completely honest with yourself and your partner and potentially begin to start resetting the way you communicate. To build on this, it is stated that one of the most common reasons for divorce is dysfunctional communication. Jun and

I are now communicating in a more constructive way, rather than a destructive one. This newfound connection came about for two reasons. One, Jun realized it was the changes he had made emotionally that were allowing us to continue living in the same house. He knew that we needed to create a healthy environment for the children, or I would make him leave. Now that only my name was on the lease (I will get to this later in the book), if he went back to speaking to me the way he used to, he would have to leave.

Two, we focused purely on the logistics of how life would be for the children. These two factors seemed to diffuse the situation and refocus us enough that we could go back to the basics. It was like a series of little resets that resulted in a major reset. We had several healing conversations and started to catch up with each other. More than just our day-to-day, but where we were emotionally. I slowly started to see the person who I had loved in the beginning of our relationship. The potential father I had fallen in love with and chosen. This was so nice because when the communication breaks down, it's easy to forget why you ever got married.

Once we both owned what our top priority was, the children, we were able to talk again. We put a pause to and stopped romanticizing how we thought our relationship should be, because all that did was make us focus on the flaws. Now our expectations purely fell onto how the other parented our kids. All the energy that was being spent on trying to either reignite or tolerate my marriage was now focused on being functional parents. I started to take responsibility for my unhealthy behavior and what pieces of myself I had been drowning out to remain in the marriage.

After I officially ended the relationship, Jun took about six months to come to terms with it. He went through a wave of emotions, which was difficult for all of us, then he finally switched. He started taking care of himself again. He made the decision to be better, to invest in Jun. He was no longer rolling through his days in a blind rage driven by frustration. He started to address his problems. From this, the dynamic completely shifted. I was able to revert back to also considering his needs, as he now cared about them too.

Back to the fundamental question that determines if you can continue to stay together in the house and cohabitate, and that is, is it really best for the children right now? It's a no-brainer that fighting in front of the children and living in a home that feels tense and strained is definitely not beneficial. That said, how do you truly quantify, as someone without a Ph.D. in child psychology and development, what is "best" for your child? I asked mine, but damn, they think ice cream for breakfast is best for them. So it's more about asking them to weigh in. Ultimately it's on us as parents, and that is hard.

**Exercise**

Tonight sit down with your children and ask them these four questions

1. What do I do that makes you feel the most loved?
2. What do I do that makes you feel the most stressed or disconnected from me?
3. What is currently causing you the most worry or concern right now?
4. Do you believe there is anything you could do that would make me love you less?

## Chapter 6

# TOGETHER AND APART

We had a family trip planned to Mammoth, which had been on the calendar since before the wildly messy breakup. At this point Jun had found a therapist, started working out, and was on medication. He was on a much needed self-care journey. Lifting weights and walking for an hour, twice a day. He was in incredible shape when we met, but with each pregnancy, we would both put on approximately twenty pounds, then I would have a baby and he wouldn't.

Over the years he had stoutly refused to work out with me, despite my encouragement, so this was a healthy progression. I knew this motivation was sparked in the hopes of winning me back, which came with some guilt, as I'd emotionally checked out. However, these feelings of guilt subsided in seeing him come back to life. He was becoming himself again, and getting in touch with the healthier side of his being. This was the push he needed to become Jun again.

The boys had settled into the narrative that Mom doesn't love Dad and he's working on himself, but mostly they were just enjoying their new and improved Dad. He was smiling and playful again. And I continued to tell them, no matter what, we would always be a family. I tried my best to keep their focus on the positives. Regardless, they were concerned that we were headed for a divorce, but for now, things were relatively calm.

The school semester was nearly over, and the boys were looking forward to going skiing. Jun loves skiing and he'd been an instructor in the past. During the pandemic, he taught the boys how to ski. It was one of the few acceptable group activities left, and fortunately, one of his passions. It's become one of my greatest pleasures to experience as a family, skiing down a mountain together. Seeing Jun happy and supportive, the boys looking to him for guidance, it was one of those pure moments you remember. We had booked a cabin with two rooms and a pullout in the living room ten months earlier, and neither Jun nor I could bear to miss out, so we were all going and all staying together.

As Jun continued to stand by his decision not to leave the family home, I had built up a little nest egg and started looking for a second place to rent. It was now mid-December and I wasn't having any luck. I wanted the new house to be reasonably priced, not run-down, and in a similar location to our current home. I was about to be a newly single mom and wanted to feel some familiarity and safety. The best option I found was a two-bedroom apartment. It was really close to their schools but with three very loud boys in one very small apartment, it was going to be chaotic. During this process of sifting through properties, I was trying to warm the boys to the idea of having two homes. I mentioned it here and there or addressed it quite directly. No matter my approach, they remained lukewarm to the idea.

A friend of mine introduced me to their real estate agent and we started viewing places immediately. She drove me from house to house but nothing in my price range fit my kids' needs. Then finally I found our second home, Regis house, and it was perfect! My budget would be very tight but if Jun continued to pay for all the extracurriculars, I could manage. I put in the preliminary application. But by the end of the week, I was dragging my feet and still hadn't provided all the needed documentation. Could I really do this? Was I making a terrible financial decision?

One day I was having a long chat with my friend Kateri, who always has something insightful to say. She asked if Jun and I are on such good terms that we are able to go on a family vacation together, couldn't we make it work living in the same house? That thought hadn't even occurred to me. I sat in silence. I was running the idea through my mind and it was starting to make sense. With the amount of extracurriculars the boys had, driving them to and from the same house would save so much time. We wouldn't have to split or double up on their belongings. And for our own schedules, it would provide both of us with a bit of freedom. The weight of being a single parent would be completely alleviated.

The layout at Regis house looked perfect. Jun would be on the bottom level with his own bedroom, living room, kitchen, and bathroom. He would be pretty much self-contained and could even access it through his own front door on the side of the house. On the second floor were two bedrooms, a full bathroom, living room, and kitchen. The top level would give me space and privacy as there was just one bedroom and a bathroom. Genius, Kateri! I left her office on Friday at 2.30 p.m., and I knew Jun would be picking up the boys from school. So I called him and asked him to bring the kids and meet me at the Regis address.

The kids loved the house, but Jun was struggling to comprehend what was happening. He wasn't committing to anything, perhaps due to his continued state of denial. But in all fairness, it was a lot for him to process all at once. I had been telling him I was leaving for six months and now I was telling him I was leaving but he could come with me. I was beginning to love this idea. It truly felt like an epiphany. I could already picture us at Regis, together and happy. Jun, on the other hand, looked like he was having an out-of-body experience. I told him that I was going to put in an application and he could make the decision for himself in his own time. I submitted the rest of the paperwork to the management before 5 p.m. and we left for Mammoth the following day. On the ride up, Jun told me he didn't want to discuss our living situation until we returned. The problem was, I received confirmation that my application had been successful a few days into our trip. I wanted to respect his need for more time so I kept it to myself and made the decision alone, renting the place solely in my name. When we returned home, I told Jun that I had signed the lease and the ball was in his court. We could stay together as a family, in one house, or separate in two.

Things then transpired in a nonverbal way. There was no big conversation, Jun just went along with it. I didn't push him to tell me what he wanted, instead I just focused on me moving. And when I started packing up my things, Jun started packing up everything. I took this as his way of saying yes, I want to live together. I didn't push him to talk about it, I just went along with it too. And together we packed up ten years of house and moved into Regis on December 24. And that following Christmas morning we woke up as a family, from our separate rooms, living together but ever so slightly apart.

## Chapter 7

# BOUNDARIES

Children know more and notice more than you think, or would like to, and don't fool yourself into thinking otherwise. They are 100 percent tuned in. Always remember that. That said, your children do not need to know about adult problems. You don't need to fill them in on more than is observable. They are children, let them be children. I constantly remind myself of this, especially because my boys are so vocal and engaged. Especially my 12 year old, he will have a conversation like he is a thirty-year-old man. Sometimes it feels like I'm chatting to a friend about my problems. But I have to stop myself because obviously he's not. They don't need details, nor to be involved in the intricacies of their parents' relationship. It is not their place to know everything, all they need is to feel safe, seen, and supported. This is why establishing healthy boundaries is so important.

Be clear and consistent with what your plans for the children are. Routinely state, "This is what you can expect." Setting clear expectations can provide a lot of security. This helps them feel safe, knowing their world isn't going to turn upside down. The longer you keep true to what you have been promising them, the more settled they will feel. They will be able to live a childhood without any of the adult realities or worries.

One of the healthiest agreements in any divorce is discretion. Your children are not the audience for your venting. Call your friend, hire a therapist, write in a journal. Do not talk to your kids about your partner. Nothing beneficial comes from them taking sides or feeling the need to do so, and it will be detrimental to their mental health. It is one of the most destructive things to come out of a divorce. It can seem like a relief, getting your point across, knowing they're watching. But can grow into a beast and destroy each partner's ability to successfully parent. And it will damage the children's relationship with both of their parents, no matter who is on the gossiping end. It is a lose-lose situation and a deal breaker when considering cohabiting.

**Exercise**

Take time to consider, discuss and agree on with your ex, what the current boundaries and expectations are for your children. What are the clear-cut rules, and what are the consequences for breaking them?

Here are ours:

THE GOTO HOUSE RULES

1. Screen time is earned using a star system, each star is worth fifteen minutes of screen time, up to a maximum of one hour a day. Currently, stars are earned for:

- Putting all personal clothing, gear and toys etc away
- Taking dishes to the sink, rinsing, and putting them in the dishwasher
- Emptying the dishwasher
- Taking out the recycling and trash
- Watering the garden
- Picking up after the dogs
- Acts of kindness
- Not complaining

2. Any disrespect in your tone, actions, or words toward either Mom or Dad results in being grounded (no electronics or playdates), for a decided length of time

3. If you name call, whether it be about your brothers or yourself, you lose a star

Expectations

1. Golden rule: If you don't have anything nice to say, don't say anything
2. Always say please and thank you
3. Sit together as a family for dinner, with no electronics, and no one leaves until everyone is finished
4. Have each others backs
5. No physical violence or violent language, ever
6. Playing sports is a privilege. If you have a genuine reason that you cannot go, a reasonable conversation is expected. No whining, crying, yelling, or complaining
7. If you are not part of the problem or the solution, do not engage in the conversation
8. Big emotions are okay, you can feel them and not take them out on anyone else
9. Hug Mom and Dad goodbye in the morning and good night at the end of the day
10. Tell Mom or Dad if anything is upsetting you, or if anyone is making you feel uncomfortable

At the end of each day, answer these questions:

1. What did you like the most today?
2. Did anything upset you today?
3. Did you do anything kind for someone else?
4. Did someone else do anything kind for you?

5. What are you particularly grateful for today?
6. What do you need from Mom or Dad?

An important habit is to regularly have logistical conversations. A shared calendar is a valuable tool in finding a routine that works for you and your specific situation. The collaboration required creates a lot of opportunities to play games, manipulate, and just wildly annoy the other person. My advice is to create as much structure around communication as you can. In our house, we have a lot of activities to schedule. To keep on top of our schedules, we have shared calendars and a whiteboard on the fridge, which has both a weekly and monthly timetable. Then on Sunday or Monday, we run through our divided jobs for the week to make sure we agree on everything and are up to date.

There's a natural intimacy and connection, not necessarily romantic, that comes from sharing the same bed. You can avoid each other all day, even using the kids as a buffer, but once you're alone and in silence, you will talk. Once I was not sharing my bed with Jun, I realized not having this moment to regroup was creating even more misunderstanding in our family.

Be honest here, has the communication broken down beyond your control? You may be at the stage where a co-parenting facilitator is necessary. A neutral third party can be a valuable tool to set you up to succeed and to address when either of you is sabotaging the situation. If you can't make this aspect work, none of it works. Take it seriously and make sure you solve this problem, because it's not going away and you can't move forward without it.

Being on the same page, in regard to discipline, can be wildly challenging when you are married. But discipline when you are separate opens the door to all kinds of crazy and misalignment. Take a moment to think about any couple you know, who do not support each other when disciplining the kids. Think about how those children act and how much peace that family enjoys...chaotic, right? Again, this may be a place where you engage with an expert to help you.

A really important one is not disagreeing with the other parent's rules or discipline in front of the children. A great practice is to agree prior to events on how you will approach them. What are the levels of punishment or reward? How do we treat each child equally? What consequences can we agree on? Taking away electronics is an easy go-to these days. However, if you are going to do this, you both have to be committed to enforcing it. It's easy to be the one to say "no iPad" and then leave for work, expecting the other parent to be the enforcer. They may not follow through if they did not agree with the punishment to begin with.

There are particular situations unique to your family, for which you will need to discuss your expectations and boundaries. Remember use values, not fears to determine your boundaries.

- Vacations: Do you go as a family, or do you go separately? What traditions will be with what parent?
- Sports games: Do you both attend and do you sit together? What if one of you has a new partner, do they attend the games? Do you all sit together?
- Dating: What do you tell each other? What do you both agree on to tell the kids?

**Exercise**

Answer the questions below, and ask your ex to do the same, then discuss together.

1. What do you like doing with the children?
2. Are there specific responsibilities you enjoy more than others?
3. What are our rules around discipline, and how do we support each other?
4. What do you need from me in regard to communication?
5. What situations do you need to have ongoing discussions about?
    a. Attendance at children's extracurricular activities
    b. School events
    c. Vacations
    d. Traditions
    e. Going out
    f. ...

Chapter 8

# NAVIGATING CONFLICT

Conflict is like the weather, it's not within your control and the best you can do is prepare for it. You and your ex presumably have your own special conflict dynamic and can predict each other's triggers and reactions. If you want to change this dynamic, you need to alter your own reactions. As parents, we must keep talking to each other, even when we are in pain and feeling betrayed. I have worked with many people who are navigating high conflict situations and learned a few things about what escalates and what de-escalates conflict.

If - not that you ever would - you want to escalate conflict, stop listening. Creating physical distance and minimizing direct communication will make the situation grow into a beast. When you stop interacting with someone on a human level, and there is nothing but empty space to fill with what can go wrong, you can quickly dehumanize them. Nothing beneficial comes from this.

There is one key to unlocking resolution when you find yourself stuck in a disagreement. The key is that until a person feels heard, they cannot listen. The challenge is when both parties don't feel heard, who listens first? The only way to come back from this vicious cycle is to start listening to each other, and one of you has to start first. Since you can only control yourself, be the first one to start listening. Get really curious, and try to understand the other person's perspective.

My favorite communication framework is Nonviolent Communication (NVC), developed by Marshall Rosenberg. It is a communication process that emphasizes empathy, understanding, and collaboration. NVC helps individuals express themselves in a way that's more likely to inspire compassion in others and likewise understand others' feelings and needs with empathy.

Here is a brief outline of Nonviolent Communication.

## FRAMEWORK

1. Observation without Evaluation:

- Start by describing the situation without evaluation, judgment, or analysis.
- For example, instead of saying "You're always late," which includes an evaluation, you might say, "I noticed you arrived after the agreed-upon time."

2. Feelings:

- Identify and express feelings without interpretation or judgment.
- Instead of saying "I feel like you're neglecting me" (which is an interpretation), you could say, "I feel sad."

3. Needs:

- Recognize and communicate the need or value causing the feeling. Needs in NVC refer to universal human needs or values, not strategies to meet those needs.
- For example, after expressing the feeling of sadness, you might add, "because I have a need for connection and shared understanding."

4. Request:

- Make a clear, concrete request for action to meet the expressed need. Ensure that the request is doable, specific, and ideally phrased in a neutral or positive tone.
- Continuing the above example, you might say, "Would you be willing to discuss how we can coordinate our schedules better?"

## TOOLS

1. Empathetic Listening:

- When listening to another person, try to hear the feelings and needs behind their words. This process might involve guessing or checking to ensure you've accurately understood their feelings and needs.
- If someone says, "You never listen to me," instead of getting defensive, you might guess the feelings and needs behind that statement, such as, "Are you feeling frustrated because you need to be heard and understood?"

2. Avoiding "Should":

- NVC promotes avoiding "should" language since it can imply wrongness or blame, which can be received as a judgment or criticism by the other party.

## CONCEPTS

1. Connecting Deeply with Others:

- The essence of NVC is to encourage a connection where both parties' feelings and needs are acknowledged and valued.

2. Recognizing Common Humanity:

- NVC suggests that all our actions are attempts to meet universal human needs. We might disagree with how someone is trying to meet these needs, but by recognizing them we increase our understanding.

- Instead of attributing our feelings to others' actions, NVC recognizes that our feelings arise from our own unmet needs and values in relation to what others do, rather than directly because of their actions.

3. Differentiating between Needs and Strategies:

- In NVC, it's important to differentiate between an individual's unmet needs (like connection, understanding, or security) from the strategies they are using to try to meet those needs.

In essence, Nonviolent Communication is a tool for creating understanding and connection, fostering compassionate interactions, and finding strategies that satisfy everyone's needs.

Last week we took our annual family photos. It was with the photographer we have used since our youngest was two. After this fun family time, Jun started calling me babe again. He hadn't done this since we moved into the new house last year. I would've said something in the moment but the kids were there. After it continued for a couple of days, I realized I needed to address it. That night after the kids had gone to bed, we were having our logistics conversation. It was going smoothly and we were hearing each other's points. Check, check! I was feeling satisfied and we were communicating well. Even in our disagreements, we were both presenting plausible compromises. Then he called me babe and I snapped. He jumped up and said he could call me whatever he likes and stormed off to his room. This was a really unnecessary outcome for what had been a very constructive and peaceful conversation. Upon reflection, I realize it was not kind on my behalf. It's easy to slip back into the habits of a relationship. Whether it be pet names or little touches. It's why boundaries are so important.

What I should have said was, over the last few days you have frequently called me babe in front of the children. This makes me feel uncomfortable, because I need authenticity. Not only for myself, but also so we do not confuse the kids. Moving forward, I would appreciate it if you would not refer to me as babe. If you continue to call me babe, I will know that you are choosing to act in a way that doesn't feel authentic to me. And we will need to discuss if a platonic relationship is something you can move forward with.

**Exercise**

To improve your ability to respond constructively, next time you feel emotionally triggered, remove yourself. Lie down and take a deep breath. Let the feelings and thoughts come up and ask yourself, what am I feeling? What do I need? Then when you feel calm, write down what the action was that triggered you, the feeling and the need. Is there something your ex could do differently next time? Then when the timing is right, calmly share this with them.

For example:

Action: He left his socks in the middle of the living room (again)
Feeling: It may have felt like anger, but what is under that anger, perhaps despair or frustration?
Need: Respect, I am not his housekeeper
Expectation: Put your socks in the hamper
Consequence: You will leave his socks on the floor to pile up and he won't have clean laundry

Start doing this for all your red button situations, getting clear on what needs are not being met and seeing if you can find solutions. Ultimately the test is if the other person is capable of listening and implementing what you are asking.

Chapter 9

# FINANCES

Money makes people do crazy things. Imagine taking the fellow parent of your children to court just so they will contribute something toward your kids' lives. Writing that makes me feel worthless because I know that's what my mom had to do. She took my dad to court for him to pay a mere $12.50 a week for me, that's $50 a month. Remember, that's New Zealand dollars. That kind of complete bull is what happens when people lose sight of their priorities or what they are fighting for.

My father stood up in court and declared his earnings, which were purely dictated in providing us with the bare minimum. He sacrificed his work and his quality of life because he didn't want to pay any meaningful amount of child support. As a parent, or even just a person, I cannot fathom doing this. He deliberately earned less money so he was not obliged to provide what's needed for his kids. They are children. They are your children. I will never understand any parent who could do this.

"Divorce is expensive" is a massive understatement. Once lawyers are in the picture and a couple is instructed to only communicate through the lawyers, miscommunication and mistrust escalate in an already broken situation. If you have really good—expensive— lawyers, it won't take long for the fear to completely derail the process. There's a lot of he said, she said and the translators are the lawyers. You will both get caught up in a whirlwind, and while you're fighting to get everything you "deserve," you'll be draining your pockets.

Finances can be a minefield, especially if you are not the main source of income for the family. Money can be and is regularly used as a weapon, especially during times of heightened emotions resulting in irrational behavior. Managing household finances under such circumstances can be challenging, but it is possible. Here are some suggestions that might help:

Create a Budget:

- Develop a new household budget that accounts for changes in income and expenses due to the separation. Include all sources of income and regular expenditures, such as mortgage/rent, utilities, groceries, insurance, childcare, etc.

Define Financial Responsibilities:

- Clearly outline who is responsible for each expense. This could be based on income or other factors that you both agree upon.

Separate Bank Accounts:

- If you haven't already, consider opening separate bank accounts for your personal expenses and possibly maintaining a joint account for shared household expenses.

Joint Account for Household Expenses:

- Consider having a joint account to which both partners contribute for household and children's expenses. Agree on how much each person will contribute and what expenses will be paid from this account.

Personal Expenses:

- Agree on how personal expenses will be managed and paid for. It might be beneficial to keep personal expenses separate.

Clear Communication:

- Maintain open lines of communication regarding finances. Regularly review the budget and expenses together to avoid misunderstandings and ensure everything is accounted for.

Set Boundaries:

- Clearly delineate what constitutes a personal expense and what constitutes a household or child-related expense. This will help in managing finances and avoiding disputes.

Emergency Fund:

- If possible, maintain an emergency fund for unexpected household expenses. Decide how much each person will contribute and how the funds will be used.

Child-Related Expenses:

- Clearly outline how child-related expenses (school fees, extracurricular activities, healthcare, etc.) will be handled and split.

Document Agreements:

- Consider putting any agreements in writing, so there is a clear reference point if any disputes arise.

Seek Professional Advice:

- It might be helpful to seek advice from a financial advisor or mediator to help structure your financial arrangements in a way that is fair and sustainable.

Be Flexible and Review Regularly:

- Be prepared to review and adjust the arrangements as necessary, especially if there are changes in income, expenses, or family needs.

Managing household finances after separation while living together can be complex. It is important to establish trust and maintain open communication. If possible, seek the support of a counselor or mediator to help navigate this arrangement and address any challenges that may arise.

Ultimately, remember you are living together because you think that is the best way to parent your children at this time. Every cent you spend on the actual divorce is subtracted from your mutual balance sheet. Stay committed to minimizing the damage to your bank account and the trust in your relationship.

**Exercise**

Develop a household budget, and include all sources of income and regular expenditures, such as mortgage/rent, utilities, groceries, insurance, childcare, etc. Clearly outline who is responsible for each expense. Agree on how much each person will contribute to the joint account and what expenses will be paid from this account.

Put all agreements in writing. Alternatively, if you are struggling to collaborate on all things financial, book a professional financial advisor or mediator to support you through this.

## Chapter 10

# DATING DYNAMICS

Once we settled in and had our own spaces, our dynamics evolved. Jun and I were in a healthy place and for me it felt comfortably platonic. And with this, came the emotional safety to start dating and meet potential partners. But, 'in theory' can often be different than, 'in reality'.

As I'm leaving the house, Jun asks if I am going on a date. I considered reminding him, we have agreed to not tell each other, but he seemed to really want to know. So I said yes, it was a date. He wanted a few more details, and against my better judgment, I gave them. When I left, he said everything was fine, and he was going to watch a movie with the boys. Initially he seemed to be keeping a handle on things, and there was silence on the home front. Then at 9.30 p.m. the text messages started coming in:

> I am sorry to bother you, I know you are on a date I really miss you but just ignore me
>
> The boys are fine
>
> The idea of it sucks
>
> My heart is breaking
>
> That's all no big deal

My interpretation of these messages was that Jun was not ready for the specifics of the dating conversation and did not have a handle on his emotions. I was home twenty minutes later to find he had been drinking, and had lost whatever grip he'd had earlier on the situation, when I left the house.

The kids had finished their movie and brushed their teeth. I kissed them goodnight and they all went to sleep. Despite hearing Jun pacing downstairs, I continued my bedtime routine and got in the shower. I was hoping he would stop. No such luck! As I was getting dressed, I heard him talking to himself, and realized he wasn't going to calm down anytime soon. I locked my door and climbed into bed. He must've heard me and started yelling things up the stairs. He was persistent. I took a deep breath and prayed the children were still asleep. I also sent out a silent thank you to their auntie Claire. She always insisted on music and chatting, and not dulling down your noise when the kids were babies, so now they can sleep through anything. Unfortunately, I could not. I was wide awake and could hear Jun banging around and smashing glasses downstairs. Not wanting things to escalate, I ventured to the living room to see what was happening.

Jun was red-faced, huffing and puffing in a fit of rage. I turn my phone's camera on for protection. Not necessarily because I thought he'd get physical, although he was throwing things, but almost as insurance. As soon as Jun saw me recording, he settled down and pretended everything was okay. I asked, "What is going on? Why are you smashing up the house?" and he suddenly decided on his story. He walked toward me, waving his bloody finger in my face, saying, "Record what you did, see this, you did this!" I couldn't quite believe he would spin things like that. Also, we both knew he was lying. How could he stand there and lie to my face like that? Knowing, I know? I told him he was crossing a line, and ran back upstairs to my room, locking the door behind me.

He came storming up the stairs and tried to open my door, but it was locked, so he started shouting again. I don't remember what he said, but there was a loud bang and the wall shook. I kept thinking, is he seriously trying to kick my door down? For some reason, I was completely calm. I don't know if it was because the boys were in the house, or if I was in shock, but I was extremely composed. He kept on kicking, getting more forceful with each blow, so I unlocked and opened the door before he caused any damage.

Still raging, he kicked the wide open door, slamming it into my bedroom wall. I told him to piss off, but he didn't. I wasn't scared of him, he had never laid a finger on me. That said, nothing like that had ever happened, and I was really worried for both of us. He was so loud that the neighbors were probably calling the police. If they turned up with Jun like this, one of us was going to get arrested, because Jun was acting unhinged and accusing me of cutting his hand.

I told him to just get out, but he wouldn't, so I left the room. He got in front of me at the top of the stairs and I pushed past him to see if the kids were still asleep, thank God, they were. He followed me down, so I went back upstairs, but he was right behind me. I tried to close my door but he kicked it, and then he just kept kicking it over and over, even though it was open. Finally the hinges came out, causing the door to dangerously hang at an angle. He was satisfied with this and went downstairs.

I waited for the sirens, but there were none. I crept downstairs and climbed into bed in the boy's room to make sure everyone was peaceful and asleep.

In the morning Jun and I didn't speak, we were both a little in shock at the damage done, and the damage escaped. This was a crucible moment, he had crossed the line in so many ways, and this had risen to an unacceptable level of verbal abuse. Could I, in all good faith, continue to live with him? I sat down and wrote out all the things he did that could never happen again. Then we sat together and discussed the situation. He was mortified with his behavior and deeply remorseful. I showed him the video of him telling me I had made his hand bleed, and he didn't remember having said it. He read through what I had written, at the end of which it stated that if he did any of these things again, he would move out. He agreed.

For some people this might have been the end of living under the same roof, but for me, I know Jun is a work in progress. He is rigorously learning to process his emotions, and thinking of me on a date with another man was too much for him to deal with. Even if we weren't living in the same house, at some stage he would have had to go through this process, and I am glad that we were able to get through it together. We now have very clear boundaries, and he knows if he crosses them again, we won't be able to live under the same roof.

When the person who once had your heart doesn't look after it anymore, and doesn't seem to care, it creates the opportunity for someone to show up and occupy that empty space. When it has been empty for years, it feels so good. It feels like the sun has come out on a gloomy day and all you want is to bask in it. I remember the feeling of being loved and seen after feeling invisible for so many years, and the emotions were overwhelming. This is human nature, we seek connection. It is shortsighted or perhaps naive to think we are okay with a lack of intimacy in the long term. Inevitably someone will show up and remind you just how unbearable it is to live without true intimacy.

For a long time, I was so focused on keeping the family together that I shut down certain innate feelings that were still inside of me. There are certain needs we will undeniably have as humans, and despite our best efforts, they will come up. But due to being so resigned with the idea of platonic love for the sake of your kids, this doesn't change what's happening around you or the people you meet, only how you perceive it.

I had considered cheating, not with a specific person, but in general. More the concept of sex with someone else as a means to an end, the end being staying married. Perhaps that sounds silly but I was committed to staying married and open to ideas. The more I explored this topic, and the more people I spoke to, I realized how common this mindset is.

For those of you in Los Angeles, you may be familiar with Ryan's Roses. Once a week on the radio, the crew call an unsuspecting spouse whose partner believes they are cheating. They pose as a new, local florist looking to promote their business by sending a dozen red roses to anyone for free. All the "florist" needs is the details of who they want to send the flowers to and a note if they wish. More often than not, the partner sends the flowers to the person they're cheating with. For years, this show has been successfully catching cheaters in their lies. Yesterday, a woman named Lisa reached out to the show and said her husband travels all the time for work. During his last trip he sent her a photo of his hotel room. It was a live photo, so she held her finger on the screen and the live picture flashed a pair of petite feet in mint-green stilettos. Turns out her husband's type is curvy blondes, which his wife is not. Apparently she had met one of his co-workers, Monica, at a work function who happened to be a curvy blonde wearing mint-green stilettos. This was when her suspicions arose, and then they were confirmed. The husband sent the roses to Monica. Ryan's Roses is entertaining for sure, but I feel so sad for these families. How, after this kind of betrayal, can the two adults operate in a healthy and constructive way? They really can't, not initially. Initially they are in survival mode. That is no place to parent from and the road back to any kind of co-parenting dynamic seems treacherous.

So that's not going to be you, you have been upfront about your marriage being over. No one is operating under false pretenses anymore. You are living with your ex. You have things in a healthy rhythm. Then, some new person has come into one of your lives, and the whole dynamic is at the risk of falling apart again! You deserve to be happy and so does your ex. In the beginning, your children are going to daydream that you will get back together, it's natural. I believe it's the way we are wired, it's what they know. It feels like everything in the universe is in place when your parents are happy and together.

After my new family dynamic became the norm, I had a one-on-one conversation with each son to let them know Jun and I would probably start dating other people. I was clear that it would not change the living situation, we would all continue to live in the same house. They each had a different reaction and were able to tell me all of their reasons as to why it was a worrying idea. I acknowledged that they wanted their parents to be together, but sometimes relationships don't work out. Their reactions were not unwarranted. The possibility of new people in their lives was daunting, especially when they occupy some of their parent's time. I tried to put myself in their shoes. And in an effort to relieve some of their worries, I said no one can have too many fantastic people in their lives. I wanted them to trust us enough to know we wouldn't choose new partners lightly. If Jun and I did date anyone, I promised they would be fantastic.

Two months later, while on a trip with the boys, I told them I'd met someone. Considering the warning, I didn't get the reaction I'd hoped for. They all shouted nonsensical statements at me for ten minutes, then the questions started to pour out. Who is he, do we know him? Do you work with him? Has he been to our house? Does Dad know? What's his name? Does he have kids? Do you know his kids? Regardless of their initial reactions, we got through it. I tried to be a vessel for their feelings, rather than reacting. Next, I called Jun and told him. He still thinks I should have told him first, but I disagree. He had broken my trust too many times, and I couldn't rely on him not to go wild and tell the children before I could. The boys and I were away for three days, which allowed them time to process it with no distractions. I thought this was optimal as Jun was able to process it alone, without the children having to witness it. His reactions were so volatile at this time, so these three days were a perfect cushion for everyone.

For a few weeks after telling them, the boys were aware of every time I was on my phone and what I was up to. Every time I left the house, they wanted to know where I was going. They'd never taken an interest in the trivialities of my calls or schedule before. Due to this, I made sure that nothing changed in regard to their time with me. I wanted them to trust that their parents dating was not going to disrupt their lives. The only one who seemed resistant and had zero interest in acknowledging or talking about anything was my eldest. He was nearly thirteen and I feel like it hit him a little differently than the other two. He can be more sensitive than most, or perhaps it's due to his age, but he seemed to take longer to process this transition.

That said, Jun and I are still trying to work out the rules around this situation. This is what we have so far:

a. The kids don't need to know the ins and outs of our adult relationships
b. We will give a ballpark estimate of expected time home unless it's relevant to activities involving the children
c. He/she is not allowed in the house yet
d. He/she is not yet allowed to come and pick us up from the house

These rules feel respectful to us at this time because of the children's ages. The rules will evolve with the needs of the family and for now they seem to be enough.

Epilogue

# TRUST THE PROCESS

When I recognized that my marriage to the father of our three sons was over, I had no plan. The only guarantee was my intent not to cause any life-changing trauma to our kids. I knew if I stayed in a relationship with my husband, I would be teaching my boys that it is okay to sacrifice your life for someone else. I would be teaching them how not to treat a woman, nor one they love. I would be teaching them what not to aspire to. How could I justify doing that? On the other hand, how could I justify being the one to break up our family? I had never wanted to bring up children in a "broken" home, and I had married a man I thought I would spend my life with. A man who I believed would protect my children before all else.

I am not naturally a patient person, but I was patient with him and patient with the process. We all learn and grow from our relationships, no matter how good or bad they may be. And I knew impatience was a fault of mine. So for Jun and our boys, I really pushed myself and I was patient. I was patient with him and he abused this. Then I was impatient with him because I gave up. The silver lining was that my giving up on him was what he needed to stop killing himself. I don't know if cohabitating with my ex is a long-term or short-term option. It is a day-at-a-time option, and so far I am really grateful that I've had the opportunity to keep working on our family together. He is the father of my children, so what is best for him is best for my children, and is best for me. My kids are learning to navigate and process their big feelings, simultaneously, so is their father. They have witnessed him start to take care of himself, workout every day and start to eat healthfully. He's even in therapy. After years of being shut down, they now have had a front row seat to how he is fighting for his family and his life, I love it.

The future holds what it will. Perhaps there will be another intimate relationship for one or both of us. Presumably this comes with not living together. Or perhaps we live in romantic solitude for many years, not entertaining anything else. For now, my commitment is to raising my children. I want them to be strong, honest, kind, loving and loved men. If there is something valuable I can do in this world, I believe that is it.

My children have so many more advantages than I did. My parents' divorce has allowed me not to make the same mistakes. No doubt, I am making different ones! But I am not alienating my children from their father. I am not making them feel responsible for the mess we have made. And both of us are there when they wake up, and when they go to sleep. All the support they need is there for them, and that's the priority.

My heart goes out to anyone going through a separation, as living together and happily ever after is what we all initially expected. With this, remember you can only control you and your actions. You have no control over the other adult, and a partner holds so much power when you share children.

Today, being a little reminiscent, I reached out to my dad. I told him I think it'd be worth getting to know me. I am living a fulfilling life with his grandchildren and appreciate the hardships of keeping a family together. My opinions are now coming from a different place, I am no longer a child, and I'd love to meet again. He opened my messages and didn't respond. I messaged him again, saying his read receipts were on, so I can tell he is choosing not to respond. To this he said, "No point." I asked him to say more and he never responded.

My heart will never truly heal from my broken relationship with my father. It is one of the reasons writing this means so much to me. From experience, I beg of you, please be kind and supportive of your ex. I know it's really hard and at times you might want to give up, but the pain your children will go through is not worth it. As adults we have gone through breakups, we have managed our pain, and we have been surprisingly resilient. Through each trauma, we have grown. So don't let your anger or ego or any kind of agenda override what's most important at this time, your kids.

I hope this book has helped you. I hope it has given you some new perspectives. The main takeaway is to stay focused on your values, to be honest and kind and remember what is important. We don't get do-overs as parents and we have a short amount of time with our children to facilitate their successes. It's a crazy world and we can't control a lot, but we can control how we treat people. Thank you for being open and receptive enough to read this book. I wish you and your family the very best.

Made in the USA
Columbia, SC
06 February 2024